M000236643

Recitations for Church Occasions

BY MELVIN WATERS

Lillenas PUBLISHING COMPANY

KANSAS CITY, MO 64141

Contents

Dedication

First, to Jesus, who saved me from a life of selfish depravity.

Second, to Betsy, my proofreader, encourager and loving wife.

Next, to my parents, Henry and Margaret Judge, who taught me to love and serve Jesus.

Last, but not least, the "members, saints, and friends" of Judge Tabernacle Holiness Church in Kinston, N.C. Much of the material in this book was gleaned from opportunities and speakers at this church between 1956 and 1970.

Using Church Recitations

It was at the Christian Booksellers Convention that an African-American dealer stopped by the Lillenas drama booth. She thumbed through all of the collections, then asked, "Do you have a book of church recitations?"

"We have them for children," I explained.

"I know," she replied, "but I want a book of adult recitations that can be used by churches of many denominational and ethnic backgrounds."

"I have nothing now, ma'am, but I'll find someone to write what you need."

Eventually, in Tulsa, Oklahoma, at a writers' conference, a young man accepted the assignment to write the recitation collection requested. Melvin Waters had just retired from the military and was immediately caught up in the challenge of such an assignment.

"I grew up in small black churches. I know exactly what you're looking for."

And well he does. Mel Waters has provided an anthology of welcomes, appreciations, announcements, eulogies, and much more. All are appropriate for churches and groups of every background.

THE PUBLISHER

Foreword

Rarely, if ever, is a former high school teacher honored by a former student by being asked to write an introduction to a book that he has written for publication. Mel Waters has so honored me.

Melvin Waters entered my English class during the turbulent '60s, determined to conquer his communicative disadvantages. His determination resulted in his mastery of standard English. During that process he explored great literature to increase his vocabulary and became mesmerized by the power of the word.

His exceptional ability soon evidenced in techniques of composition. His love for words both spoken and written became the center of his life and ultimately livelihood.

Recitations for Church Occasions will provide a ready source of appropriate selections for anyone who does not have the time to formally prepare salient remarks. Materials included are designed for making the speech short and to the point.

DIANA D. KORNEGAY

Welcome
to a
New Pastor

The office of the undershepherd or pastor is one of high responsibility and seriousness. The pulpit committee undertook the pastoral selection with much prayer and concern for the spiritual welfare of this congregation.

Today, we celebrate the arrival of one we believe is God's choice to lead [church name]. Please join with me in welcoming our new undershepherd, Pastor [name].

It is with great joy and expectation that we welcome our new pastor today. He attended [schools] and served as [past offices] with great distinction. However, his most important distinction is that he loves God and will pass that love on to this congregation.

He is married to [wife's name], and they have [number of children and names].

Please join me in welcoming our new pastor, Rev. [name], and his family.

The man who stands behind the sacred desk as pastor has many awesome responsibilities. He must not only preach but also be able to counsel, guide, and reconcile—just to mention a few duties.

The man God has selected for this task is capable of each duty, yet is humble in demeanor. He realizes that it is the "treasure in earthen vessels" who empowers the undershepherd to lead the flock.

He was born again [salvation date]. He was educated at [schools]. He has served [list past pastorates and duties]. However, his most important qualification is that God has sovereignly sent him here to be our pastor.

Please stand and join with me in giving a hearty welcome to Pastor and Mrs. [names].

The man whom God selected to lead this great congregation was born [birth date], was born again on [salvation date], and was called to ministry on [time period of ministry call]. He is the husband of [wife's name] and the father of [children's names].

He has served [past pastorates and duties]. He was educated at [list of schools/colleges].

Will you join me in a warm welcome to Rev. [name] and his family.

This is a joyful time for [name of church]. It is the result of many hours of seeking God in prayer for the right man to lead this congregation. We believe the man God has sent us is more than capable of leading this congregation.

He has a godly legacy of service and scholarship. He has served [list of past pastorates and duties] and was educated at [list of schools]. He is a leader who is a servant.

He is the husband of [wife's name] and the father of [children's names]. Most importantly, he is a son of God. He was born again [date of salvation] and called to the ministry [time period of ministry call].

We believe he is God's man to lead this great congregation. Please welcome our new pastor, Rev. [name], and his family.

Although the pulpit committee did the administrative work, we all believe that it was God who gave us our new pastor. He is a servant/leader with a great love for God. He has served at [past pastorates and duties] with great distinction. He is married to [wife's name] and is the father of [children's names]. He was educated at [list of schools].

He met Jesus [date of second birth] and was called into the ministry [date of ministry call].

Please join me in extending a hearty welcome to our new pastor, Rev./Bro. [name], and his family.

Greetings in the wonderful name of Jesus to the members and friends of [church name]. We sincerely want to thank the members of the pulpit committee for their ceaseless prayers and tireless efforts in the pastoral selection.

First a few words of introduction. Pastor [name] was born [date, place, parents]. He was born again [date] and was called to the ministry [date/period]. He is the husband of [wife's name] and the father of [children's names and ages].

His previous positions of service include [list of pastorates and duties]. In each place, he has brought honor to the name of Jesus.

Please stand and join me in welcoming our new pastor, Brother [name], and his family.

Pastor Appreciation

The Bible tell us that "elders . . . are worthy of double honor" (1 Tim. 5:17). Today it is our pleasure to fulfill that biblical text by showing our appreciation for Pastor [name].

He has labored diligently in the fields of our lives. Because of his leadership, we are better Christian servants. Through his ministry, God has called several from our flock into full-time service. The influence of Pastor [name] has extended from our local Judea, into Samaria and around the world.

Our words and gifts fall far short in expressing our full appreciation. Yet, we humbly present them to you, Pastor [name], as a token of our love.

Will the congregation please rise and give a hearty applause of appreciation to Pastor [name].

Through the years, you have served with great honor and distinction. Today, we pause to show our appreciation to you, Pastor [name]. You were sent by God to us "for such a time as this."

Regardless of the text, your sermons are always laced with the love of God. You have led us gently like a shepherd. You indeed reflect the Good Shepherd.

We pray that the events of this day will be a blessing to you, as you continue to be a blessing to us as our pastor.

This appreciation service is dedicated to a man who leads us gently like the Good Shepherd. Pastor [name] has served this congregation [years]. In those years, God has wonderfully blessed us.

[Review such issues as the following: church growth, missions growth, members called to full-time service, young people's programs, etc.]

Pastor, we love you and appreciate you, and pray God's continued blessing on your life.

Today we honor a man of God who has humbly served us for [years]. He is an honorable man of impeccable character.

Pastor, we realize that your ultimate reward will come from God. However, we present these gifts to you from our hearts as an expression of appreciation for your wonderful service.

We give honor to God that all of you could join us in giving thanks for our pastor. It is one thing to be a leader; yet quite another to be a servant leader. Our pastor is a servant leader. He has shown us what Jesus is like both in word and in deed.

Please stand and join with me in an applause of appreciation for Pastor [name].

A pastor is a man called of God to be an undershepherd to a local congregation. He is one who embodies the love of God and practical leadership traits. We are blessed to have such a man as pastor.

Today, in verbal and physical expression, we give honor to Pastor [name].

Love and appreciation are more than just verbal expressions of gratitude. They are tangible tokens shown to someone worthy of honor. Such a person is our pastor.

He has served us faithfully for [years]. He has led us like the Good Shepherd to green pastures of God's Word and Christian service.

Today is your day, Pastor! May God continue to use you mightily for the "equipping of the saints" to be His ministers.

A pastor is one of five gifts given to the church for the equipping of the saints, according to Eph. 4:11. The saints of this church pause today to show our appreciation for our equipper.

For [years] he has lovingly served this congregation with honor and distinction. Our service to God has been enhanced under his able leadership.

Pastor, today's activities can only in small part show our real appreciation. We love you, we honor you, we appreciate you . . .

For [number] years, Pastor [name] has labored in our vineyard. As an equipper of the saints, he has epitomized Eph. 4:11. His ministry has sent out many workers to serve other congregations near and far.

Pastor, may the words of our mouths and the gifts of our hands encourage you to even greater exploits in God. Please stand and join me in honoring this servant of the Most High God!

Engagement Announcements

According to God, marriage is an honorable institution. Engagement or betrothal (Luke 1:18-19) precedes marriage and is a time of serious contemplation and anticipation. In fact, in Bible days it was a binding covenantal relationship. We say this to highlight the seriousness of the engagement period.

This couple is fully aware of God's view of engagement and marriage. On the occasion of their announcement, I joyfully present to this congregation: [name of prospective bride] and [name of prospective groom].

Engagement is a time of joy and anticipation of future matrimony. This church endorses such godly relationships sanctioned by the Holy Spirit. We pray God's greatest blessings on [name of prospective bride] and [name of prospective groom] as today they announce their engagement to be married.

Today, I am honored to announce an engagement in our congregation. Engagement is a wonderful period of preparation for married life. God is pleased because marriage is a similitude of the relationship between Christ and the Church.

With great joy, the parents and I proudly announce the engagement of [name of prospective bride] and [name of prospective groom].

God has given us marriage as a wonderful picture of Christ and the Church. Before marriage, engagement is given as a period of preparation for that picture. It is a time to pray, plan, and seek to understand the mystery of Jesus' love.

Today, [name both sets of parents] and I gladly announce the engagement of [name of prospective bride] and [name of prospective groom].

Today, with great pleasure, I join with [name both sets of parents] in announcing the engagement of [name of prospective bride] and [name of prospective groom].

Will the congregation please stand and join me in prayer. Dear God, we thank You for marriage, and we pray Your wisdom on [name of prospective bride] and [name of prospective groom] as they enter this wonderful period of engagement.

Engagement is a wonderful time of anticipation and marital preparation. This church is committed to the perpetuation of God-honoring families. Such families are indeed a reflection of Christ and the Church.

On this occasion, [name both sets of parents] and I joyfully announce to this congregation the engagement of [name of prospective bride] and [name of prospective groom].

Engagement, and the subsequent marriage, represent a divine progression of God's intention for mankind. In marriage we see the perpetuation of the race and a picture of Jesus and the Church. This church is dedicated to the preparation and perpetuation of godly families.

With that preamble, [name both sets of parents] and I proudly announce the engagement of [name of prospective bride] and [name of prospective groom] to be married.

Wedding Announcements

Believing that God has brought them into one another's lives, [name of bride] and [name of groom] request your presence at their wedding on [date], at [time], at [name of church].
The reception will follow at/in [place].

With joy and happiness, [name of bride] and [name of groom] request you join them as they come together in holy matrimony on [date], at [time], at [place].
The reception will follow at/in [place].

Praise God! Your presence is requested as wedding bells ring for [name of bride] and [name of groom] on [date], at [time], at [place].

[name of bride] and [name of groom] request you be their special guest at their wedding on [date], at [place]. Reception to follow at the church.

Believing God has predestined them to be joined together in holy matrimony, [name of bride] and [name of groom] request you join them in celebrating this sacred event on [date], at [time], [place].
Reception to follow at/in [place].

In celebration of the union of Christ and the Church, [name of bride] and [name of groom] request your presence at their wedding on [date], at [time], [place].
Reception will follow at/in [place].

Believing God has brought them into one another's lives to be married, [name of bride] and [name of groom] request your attendance at their wedding at [time, place], on [date].

The reception will follow at/in [place].

You are cordially invited to attend the wedding celebration of [name of bride] and [name of groom] on [date], at [time, place].

Reception to follow at/in [place].

Your presence is requested at the marriage celebration of [name of bride] and [name of groom] on [date], at [time, place].

Reception following the wedding at/in [place].

In fulfillment of God's institution that "the two become one flesh," [name of bride] and [name of groom] invite you to join them at their wedding ceremony [date, time, place].

Reception following at/in [place].

In joyful celebration of holy matrimony, [name of bride] and [name of groom] request your presence on [date], at [time, place].

Reception at [time, place].

Believing marriage is a picture of Christ and the Church, [name of bride] and [name of groom] invite you to join them as they are joined in holy matrimony.

Ceremony and reception will be held [date], at [time, place].

New Baby
Introductions

The Bible says in Ps. 127:3 that "children are a gift from the LORD" (NCV). With great pleasure, I introduce to you a gift born to [parent's name]: [baby's name], born [date].

Today it is a most wonderful pleasure to introduce the newest member of this congregation. He [She] was born to [parents' names] on [date], weighing in at [birth weight]. Please stand with me and join in a welcoming prayer for [baby's name].

Prayer: Dear Lord, thank You for the safe delivery of [baby's name]. We speak the greatest blessings of Jesus on this baby. We commit ourselves to pray for and help spiritually nurture this new life. Guide the parents as they exhibit the love of our Heavenly Father to this child. Thank You, Lord, for Your grace in raising this baby in "the nurture and admonition of the Lord" (Eph. 6:4, KJV).

James 1:17 declares that "every good and perfect gift is from above." Today, I am very pleased to introduce one of God's most recent and perfect gifts to [parent's names] and this church. He [She] arrived on [birthday], weighing [birth weight]. Please join me in welcoming our newest member, [baby's name].

Jesus loved the little children when He was on earth. At one point He stated that we must come to Him like little children. What does that mean? Well, it means we must all trust and depend upon Him for our substance and very existence. Today, we celebrate the physical birth of one dear to the heart of Jesus . . . and to us.

[Baby's name] was born to [parent's names] on [birthday], weighing [birth weight]. Ladies and gentlemen, with great delight, I introduce to you [baby's name].

From the day God inaugurated the family in the Garden of Eden, procreation was His order to Adam and Eve for the perpetuation of the human race. Our presence here today testifies to the continuation of that divine edict. Consequently, our prayers and best hopes go out to these very happy parents and relatives on the occasion of this formal introduction.

He [She] was born [birthday], weighing [birth weight]. [Parents' names] and I take great pleasure in introducing to you [baby's name].

One of God's most precious gifts to the human race is the gift of children. They carry our dreams, our hopes, and the Christian faith from one generation to another.

Today, [parents' names] and I are honored to introduce to you one of God's most recent gifts to us, born on [date], weighing [weight], to [parents' names]. Will the congregation please welcome [baby's name].

Death and Funeral Announcements

On [date], [deceased's name] entered into the presence of the Lord. Our prayers go out to the dear family in this time of loss. May the support of the family of faith uphold and encourage them in the coming weeks and months.

[Deceased's name] will be funeralized on [date], at [place], with [minister's name] officiating.

The population of heaven was increased by one on the occasion of the passing of [deceased's name] on [date]. Though our hearts ache at the loss, we rejoice that all who know Jesus will see him [her] again. We do not weep "as others who have no hope" (1 Thess. 4:13, NCV). Our hope is in Jesus, who will one day reunite all those who believe in Him.

We commit ourselves to help the family during this difficult period. The funeral will be held at [place], at [time], with [minister's name] officiating.

Jesus took the sting of death on Calvary, yet there is still a hurt when death takes a dear loved one. [Deceased's name] was ushered into the presence of God on [date]. We rejoice and mourn in this time of our loss and heaven's gain.

Our prayers and ministry of practical help go out to the family. They are the wonderful testimony to the godly heritage of [deceased's name].

Please join [minister's name] in memorializing [decreased's name] on [date], at [place].

[Deceased's name] passed through the portals of heaven on [date]. We sense a great feeling of loss yet joy for heaven's gain. Death is a curse that resulted from Adam's sin, so we give no credit to it. It represents a transition from earth to glory for the believer. Again, we rejoice that [deceased's name] is in God's presence.

We will eulogize [deceased's name] on [date], at [time], at [place], with [minister's name] officiating.

[Minister's name] will preside at the funeral of [deceased's name], who passed into eternity on [date]. The burial will follow at [cemetery name].

Our hearts reach out to the family in words and deeds of encouragement during this time.

[Date of death], [deceased's name] went to sleep on earth and woke up in heaven. Heaven's population increased though ours decreased. However, in the knowledge that [deceased's name] knew God, we rejoice that we believers will see him [her] again.

We pray for the family's strength in this period of adjustment to this loss. You were blessed to have such a godly family member.

The funeral will be held on [date], at [time, place], with [minister's name] officiating.

Eulogies

When we move from one earthly residence to another, we normally send our friends a change of address card. On that card, we list our new street and city name. Well, [deceased's name] moved from his [her] earthly home to the streets of gold in New Jerusalem City on [date].

There is no housing shortage there, for he [she] has his [her] own mansion. There is no shortage of light, for the Lord Jesus (the Lamb) lights the city. There is no crime there, for righteousness is the order of the day.

Though such words of prior elegance cannot lessen the hurt we feel at the loss of our friend, we believers have reason to cheer. That reason is that we will one day see him [her] again in what Mahalia Jackson called "That Great Gittin' Up Morning."

I thank God that I had the privilege of knowing [deceased's name]. Words of tribute seem appropriate yet hollow at a time like this. So we will let the record of my friend's life speak for itself: From early years, he [she] served God with great distinction. He [She] ministered in the following offices with great dignity and diligence: [list church offices held].

Two loves could always be seen in his [her] life: a love for God and a love for people. For such a heritage, we are much richer for having known such a saint.

For those of us who know Jesus, death is a transition from gloom to glory. The gloom is this earthly veil of tears from which we shall all pass one day. The glory is the presence of Jesus, who died for us and yet lives.

[Deceased's name]'s life represented the "incarnational presence" of Jesus and the finest of Christian tradition. Mere words cannot fully express the eternal impact of a life lived for the sake of others.

So to the dearly departed, we say not good-bye, but see you later.

For the believer, this earthly sojourn is at best a preparation for eternity. [Deceased's name] prepared well by living a life reflecting a personal knowledge of Jesus. Our sense of hurt and loss must be seen in the light of heaven's gain. As King David said upon the loss of his son, "I will go to him, but he will not return to me" (2 Sam. 12:23). So we can say about this loss, we can go to him [her]—if we know Jesus.

Dear friend, though we will see you again, we miss you now. Our blessings go with you as you reside with God. Praise the Lord! We shall see you again.

I met [deceased's name] in [year]. We shared such sweet fellowship in Jesus. His [Her] kind smile and words of encouragement brought light to otherwise dark days. Though our loss is heaven's gain, I shall deeply miss my dear friend.

[Deceased's name] now resides where pain and suffering is a thing of the past, and joy and gladness eternally last. I could list his [her] earthly accomplishments, but that would not be what he [she] would want us to do. Knowing [deceased's name] as well as I did, I can most assuredly tell you what he [she] would say to you today.

[Deceased's name] would ask you the following questions: "Is it well with your soul?" "Will you meet me in the morning?" and lastly, "Is Your Name Written in the Lamb's Book of Life?" You see, the answer to these three questions will determine whether you will see him [her] again.

I now end with these words:
Farewell, dear friend;
Death is not the end,
For early in the morning
We shall see you again.

I knew [deceased's name] for [number of years]. His [Her] love for God was as evident outside the church as it was inside. I will not try to make him [her] more in death than he [she] was in life. I will just say that if all of us lived for God as he [she] did, this world would be a much better place.

I encourage the family to keep on, not in your own strength but in the power of God's might.

Today we celebrate the homegoing of [deceased's name] on [date].

Though we feel grief, hurt, and a deep sense of loss, there is rejoicing in heaven. That celebration exceeds any party ever held on earth. Moreover, the greatest tribute we could ever pay to [deceased's name] would be to meet him [her] there.

His [Her] life constantly reflected the love of Jesus. Because of Christ's love, he [she] knew no strangers, only fellow Christians or potential Christians. We are much richer today because [deceased's name] walked among us.

So let us not "grieve as others do who have no hope" (1 Thess. 4:13, NRSV). For we who know God will see [deceased's name] again, maybe sooner—maybe later.

Eulogy Poetry

Farewell, old friend.
We walked together many a year;
The joy of ages past we shared;
We laughed, we cried, we did our best.
Today is not a final good-bye,
For we shall one day meet again
In a place where we will never depart;
For the sweetness of God shall be ours.
So until we meet again,
Farewell, old friend.

No good-bye, but see you later.
Heaven's call is something greater.
There no sickness, death, or pain
But better still the Lord we gain.

One day in heaven
    when we wake up,
No longer to drink
    of earth's bitter cup;
But in His presence
    to live always,
With no more night
    but glorious days.

A sweet letter he wrote
   on his tablet of love—
A life lived for others
   by God's grace above.
A picture of Christ
   he daily showed us all;
Now in His presence
   as he answered the call,
But one day soon
   we will meet again,
Never to depart
   as God welcomes us in.

Today we pause to ponder,
   with kind words from the heart
That recall sweet memories
   of loved ones that depart.
Words of reflection
   as a movie that is run;
But even greater still,
   our friend lives with the Son.

Homecoming Welcome

On behalf of the pastor and staff, I welcome you to our annual homecoming services. Many of you have come from distances far and near. I thank God for His traveling mercies and bountiful grace on your behalf. I pray you will enjoy today's program, renew old acquaintances and make many new ones.

Again, welcome to our homecoming services.

Welcome to our annual homecoming services. The pastor and staff are delighted that you could join us today. We encourage you to join in as we give glory to God. Truly, He has blessed us to return here on this great occasion.

Welcome home and God bless you.

Welcome, visitors and friends from far and near, to our annual homecoming celebration. The pastor, staff, and members have been praying for your safe arrival and enjoyment. So join in as we sing, praise, and bless the Lord.

Again, welcome home.

It is such a delight to welcome you all to our annual homecoming services. The pastor, staff, and members stand available to make sure you enjoy this event.

So, make yourself at home and join us as we give glory and honor to Jesus, "our King of kings and Lord of lords."

Welcome, welcome, welcome!

Coming to a homecoming service is a special time. It is a time of meeting old friends and making new friends. On behalf of the pastor, staff, and members, I welcome you all to our annual homecoming services.

So get involved in the service and again, WEL-COME!

Welcome one and all to our homecoming service. We are thankful for your safe arrival. Please join with us as we give glory to God.

Have a great day . . . and again, WELCOME!

Taking
the Offering

The essence of Christianity is to receive from God and then give to others. Today, we have such an opportunity to give. The Bible says, "It is more blessed to give than to receive" (Acts 20:35, KJV). Please join with us in blessing others as we give to the Lord.

Giving is as much a part of worship as other parts of the service. Please join with us now in worshipful giving to the Lord. To Him be glory and honor in our giving.

Jesus loved us so much that He gave. Because of His example, we now have an opportunity to do the same. Our giving is in the form of material goods, yet it has an eternal significance. We pray God will return a hundred-fold for your generous gifts today.

Giving reflects the nature of God. He gave us His Son, and Jesus gave us life. Although, we could never give to such a magnitude, we can bless others as God has blessed us. Our gifts help insure that the message of Jesus is spread. Join us now as we participate in the worship of giving.

Jesus' gift gave us eternal life. We can help others know Him through our giving. Please seek God as to what He would have you give to help spread the message of eternal life. Thank you for your generosity.

This offering will help spread the message of the gospel. It is a small token of our appreciation to God and our love for others. Please join with us as we bless God in our giving.

We can never repay God for His bountiful love to us. However, we can, by our generosity, help others to know of His love. Join with us now as we give so that others may experience the life-giving power of Jesus.

Replies to
Introductions

Until Mr. [Mrs.; Miss] [name] called my name, I was wondering whom he [she] was describing. Truly, such an introduction is apt for a king. I appreciate and applaud such gracious words.

If Mr. [Mrs.; Miss] [name] speaks as eloquently as he [she] introduces, I would much rather hear him [her] than myself. I think we should applaud him [her] for such a wonderful introduction.

Thank you, Mr. [Mrs.; Miss] [name], for such a gracious introduction. Such splendid words are appreciated and shall be long remembered.

I would like to have a cassette of that introduction. I plan to play it when I have a down day or need a brighter one. Thank you for such kind words. I pray that my brief comments will fit such splendid rhetoric.

I humbly thank you for such kind words. As I listened, I was motivated to pray that I would be equal to the introduction. Please pray with me that my subsequent words will be divinely empowered to affect eternal change.

I appreciate and applaud such an introduction. I pray that my comments will be as much a blessing to you as these words have been to me.

If an award was given for introductions, that one would win. Thank you for such courteous words. May these next few comments be as polite as that introduction.

Thank you for such a marvelous preamble. All those fine comments are the result of the love and blessings of an awesome God. To Him be glory, honor, and praises.

Thanks for such a great introduction. Now, please let me quickly get into my speech before I start believing it.

Speaker
Appreciation
Comments

Mr. [Mrs.; Miss] [name], thank you for such a wonderful address. We have all been challenged and moved by your inspired words. We encourage you to continue spreading the word. God bless and keep you.

Thank you, Mr. [Mrs.; Miss] [name], for your oration. We were moved and delighted by your powerful words. May such words engender change and betterment to future hearers.

Such dynamic words as we have just heard hold the seeds of greatness. I appreciate Mr. [Mrs.; Miss] [name]'s comments and pray that they will germinate in the soul of each hearer. Only then will change be affected and mighty exploits be accomplished. Again, thank you, Mr. [Mrs.; Miss] [name].

Thank you for such potent words, Mr. [Mrs.; Miss] [name]. We have been motivated and mobilized by your challenge. Please stay the course and keep on telling your story. Again, thank you!

Thank you, Mr. [Mrs.; Miss] [name], for such powerful words. Such a message cannot be easily ignored. We all will have to deal with your challenge in the days to come. I pray that each of us will heed your call and diligently deal with the tenets of your words.

Such words as we have heard paint a tapestry that cannot be ignored. Thank you, Mr. [Mrs.; Miss] [name], for such a wonderful speech. We encourage you to continue the work that God has begun in you.

Mr. [Mrs.; Miss] [name], thank you for such an eloquent presentation. These inescapable truths have challenged us to higher heights. May you be strengthened as you continue spreading your message.

Mr. [Mrs.; Miss] [name], thank you for such a great speech. The seeds of positive change were planted by your words. Please keep on blessing others with your powerful admonishments.

Scholarship Presentations

We thank God for the work He has done in the lives of these young people. It is by His power that their studying and academic toils have reaped these scholarships.

The knowledge that gained these scholarships will truly prosper these students as they apply God's wisdom to their academic knowledge.

The Bible says that people "will enjoy the fruit of their deeds" (Isa. 3:10). Today, these scholarship recipients will receive some of the "fruit" of their academic labors. These scholarships are by no means an ultimate reward, but they represent the toils of past labors and the forerunner of future challenges.

I am very pleased to present the following scholarships to:

[list recipients]

Today we celebrate the presentation of scholarships to these deserving students. Their many hours of studying and hard work have reaped a reward that will allow their legacy of excellence to continue. Our prayer for them is that they continue to recognize that God is the true Giver of these scholarships—as well as knowledge and wisdom.

I am honored to present the following scholarships to:

[list recipients]

The Bible declares that all good and perfect gifts come from God. While earthly scholarships may not be perfect, they are good. They represent the rewards of many hours of study and hard work. I am sure these students can testify that the many papers, examinations, oral quizzes, etc., presented some challenges.

However, today we celebrate their victory over these challenges and their entry into a higher realm of study.

Ladies and gentlemen, with great pleasure and honor, I present the following scholarships to:

[list recipients]

A scholarship is the harvest from seeds of study and hard work. It is one way in which God rewards the fruit of our labor. These scholarship recipients can be rightly proud of their accomplishments. Their sacrifices of time and temporal pleasures have reaped a benefit of future rewards.

We thank God for the blessings of the past and invoke faith for a future that will bring glory to His name.

I present to you the following scholarship winners:

[list recipients]

Mere words cannot express the joy that we all feel for these scholarship award winners. They labored long and hard, and God is today rewarding their efforts.

We pray God's continued blessings on these students as they move into their next level of higher learning. May God bless their future labors as He has their past.

Ladies and gentlemen, I gladly present the following scholarship award winners:

[list recipients]

Ultimately, God is the Giver of all gifts. He repays the diligent for their work. These scholarships are God's way of rewarding your devotion to hard study and your quest for academic excellence.

By God's grace, you met and conquered all challenges. The past is a wonderful historical legacy that you can reflect upon with pride. Yet, the future awaits with equal challenges. In faith we believe you will meet its challenges.

I joyfully present the following scholarship award winners:

[list recipients]

Welcomes:
USHERS' APPRECIATION SERVICE

On behalf of Pastor [name], our board, and the members of [church's name], I welcome you to the Ushers' Appreciation Service.

The value of ushers cannot be stated in mere words. They are usually the first person you meet when you arrive at church and the last one you see when you leave. They are the greatest in Jesus' eyes because they are servants in the purest sense of the word.

Please relax, praise and worship God for the wonderful ushers He has given this church.

Again, welcome to our Ushers' Appreciation Service.

Pastor [name], the church board, and the membership welcome you to our Ushers' Appreciation Day.

Most of us take for granted the hard work done by the ushers in our church. What we see in the church service is only a small portion of what they do for the church. Even before they arrive at church, they bathe the service in prayer and seek God's direction for their day. After the service, they help clean up the sanctuary and are often the last ones to leave.

The Bible tells us to give "honor to whom honor is due" (Rom. 13:7, NRSV). Today we honor our servant ushers to the glory of God.

Again, welcome to our Ushers' Appreciation Day!

On behalf of Pastor [name] and the members of this church, we welcome you to our Ushers' Appreciation Service.

Ushers are some of the most visible representatives of our churches. They train hard and work hard to make the worship service God-centered and without distraction. Today, we show our appreciation, realizing that ultimately God will give them their greatest reward.

Once more, welcome to our Ushers' Appreciation Service.

Pastor [name] and the members of this church welcome you to our annual Ushers' Day Service.

Ushers are kind of like the Alpha and the Omega. They are usually the first ones you see as you get to the church and the last ones you see before you leave. In a deeper sense, though, they represent the greatness of God because they are the "servants of all." This service is set aside to show them just how much we appreciate them for serving God by serving us.

Again, welcome one and all.

On behalf of Pastor [name] and the members of this church, I welcome you to our Ushers' Appreciation Service.

What do you see when you envision an usher? Usually someone who greets you at the door with a warm smile and a handshake. Or perhaps someone in a white uniform or a black suit who helps you find a seat.

While these are the usual stereotypes, ushers are much more than these images project. They are children of God actively fulfilling Jesus' orders to be servants of all. We are all the beneficiaries of their obedience to God.

Ushers, we salute you . . . ladies and gentlemen, we again welcome you.

On behalf of Pastor [name] and the members of this church, I welcome you to our Ushers' Appreciation Service.

Today we honor "the proud, the few," the ushers of this church. Like the marines of the military, they serve with grace and diligent distinction. From the halls of the foyer to the shores of the baptistery, they bring honor and glory to the name of Jesus.

We thank God that you have joined us in this appreciation service, and again we welcome you.

Welcomes:
CONVENTION/CONVOCATION

On behalf of Bishop [name] and the host church [church's name], I welcome you to our [number] annual convention/convocation.

We thank God for bringing you from vast distances to join us in praise and worship to God. Though we have much business to transact, our prime purpose will always be that of glorifying God.

We ask God's wisdom and guidance for this entire convention/convocation.

Again, welcome and be blessed.

On behalf of Bishop [name] and the officials of this convention/convocation, I joyfully welcome you all.

God has wonderfully blessed us from last year until now. This series of meetings will purpose to bless the Lord in return. In our business meetings, in our fellowship, in our mealtimes . . . we will bless the Lord.

Again, welcome to this convention/convocation.

I welcome you on behalf of Bishop [name] and the officials of this convention/convocation. We are here to serve you.

Our purpose is to give glory to God in all we do. Whether in worship, business, or fellowship, we will honor God. Your presence testifies to your desire to do the same.

Again, welcome to this convention/convocation.

We are delighted to have you all here. On behalf of Bishop [name] and the convention/convocation officials, I welcome you.

This convention/convocation is committed to lifting up the name of Jesus in all that is done. God has given us the privilege of taking His gospel to the nations. We gather here to thank Him for the victories of the past and beseech Him for even greater exploits by His Spirit. Your presence demonstrates your dedication to this future.

Again, welcome to this convention/convocation.

On behalf of Bishop [name] and the convention/convocation officials, I joyfully welcome you to our [number] annual convention/convocation.

We are here to give glory to God. In our fellowship and business meetings, we will glorify God. We also pause to thank God for safely bringing each of you to this meeting. He is a good God.

Again, welcome to this convention/convocation.

Welcome to our [number] annual convention/convocation on behalf of Bishop [name] and convention/convocation officials.

We thank God for what He has done through this organization over the past year. We envision a fruitful future of ministry to society and to the world. You will be blessed by the events of this week.

Again, welcome to our convention/convocation.

Mortgage-
Burning
Ceremonies

Welcome to our mortgage-burning ceremony. [Number] years ago, we believed God and bought this beautiful facility. Since then, God has enabled us to pay off the loan. For that, we praise God!

We again commit ourselves to our original purpose of glorifying God. As much as we like this facility, it is only temporal at the most. However, the persons saved as a result of our ministry will spend eternity with God.

We thank God that He has given us the funds to pay off our mortgage. This mortgage-burning ceremony is a testimony to the faithfulness of God and our members.

Buildings will pass away, but human souls are eternal. This facility has served as a base for many that have come to know Jesus. We thank God for those He has blessed through ministry in this building and from this building.

We burn this mortgage knowing that, according to God's Word, those who come to know Jesus will not burn.

On behalf of the pastor and members of this church, we welcome you all to this mortgage-burning service.

Mortgage burnings signify the faithfulness of God through His servants to a ministry. God surely will "supply all your need according to his riches in glory by Christ Jesus" (Phil. 4:19, KJV). However, He often uses delegated, benevolent givers to literally supply the money.

Today's ceremony honors those obedient givers who believed in and supported the vision of this church.

Today's mortgage burning represents a change of ownership from the bank to the people of God. As people of God, we accept the stewardship of this beautiful facility. We say stewardship because God alone is the Owner.

We are blessed that you came to share this day with us. Many of you have sacrificed and labored to make this day possible. To you we express our grateful appreciation and dedication to remain faithful stewards of this property.

Welcome to our mortgage-burning service. God has blessed us through the faithful laborers of this church. To those laborers, we express our appreciation for their obedience.

This mortgage burning represents our desire to better use God's provisions to reach more of the lost. Buildings last for only a few years, but men's souls are eternal. May God use ministry from these facilities to bring men to eternal life in Him.

Deacon
Installation
Ceremonies

We are delighted that you have joined us for this deacon's installation program. True deacons serve at the behest of God. They are mighty men of God and, like the biblical Philip, are committed totally to the cause of Christ and secondarily to serving their local church.

Welcome to our program.

Welcome to our deacon's installation ceremony. From the first century until this day, deacons have provided service and leadership to the Church of God. They are often unseen and more often unappreciated, but they serve anyway. Theirs is a call from God, and they diligently honor that call.

Again, welcome to our deacon's installation ceremony.

Deacons are the backbone of the church and the epitome of servanthood and leadership. Today, we take great pleasure in the induction of new deacons into our church. We offer thanks to God for them and pray God's grace and power in their future tenure of service.

We also thank God for your presence at this wonderful occasion.

Throughout church history, deacons have blessed the Body of Christ by their diligence and commitment to God. Today, that tradition of blessing continues as we dedicate these candidates to the office of a deacon.

Thank you for joining us and welcome to these ceremonies.

The deacon candidates before you have proven themselves as spiritual servants for the cause of Christ. As a result of their commitment and diligence, they will today be dedicated to the office of deacon. We thank them for their past excellence and pray for their bright future in the office of church deacon.

We also welcome you all for attending this wonderful event.